○ **IDentity Series** ○

Finding Success as a Returning Veteran or Military Student

Phil McNair and Fred Stielow

PEARSON

Boston • Columbus • Indianapolis • New York • San Francisco • Upper Saddle River
Amsterdam • Cape Town • Dubai • London • Madrid • Milan • Munich • Paris • Montreal   Toronto
Delhi • Mexico City • Sao Paulo • Sydney • Hong Kong • Seoul • Singapore • Taipei • Tokyo

Editor in Chief: Jodi McPherson
Acquisitions Editor: Katie Mahan
Development Editor: Charlotte Morrissey
Editorial Assistant: Erin Carreiro
Senior Managing Editor: Karen Wernholm
Senior Production Project Manager: Tracy Patruno
Director of Marketing: Margaret Waples
Executive Marketing Manager: Amy Judd
Text and Cover Designer: Kathryn Foot
Image Managers: Mike Lackey and Rachel Youdelman
Procurement Specialist: Megan Cochran
Project Management and Composition: Jouve
Printer/Binder: Courier/Kendallville
Cover Photo: lantapix/Shutterstock

Many of the designations by manufacturers and sellers to distinguish their products are claimed as trademarks. Where those designations appear in this book and the publisher was aware of a trademark claim, the designations have been printed in initial caps or all caps.

All photos © Shutterstock except: page 1 © Zimmytws/Fotolia, page 6 Troops to Teachers, page 7 National Guard Bureau, page 9 The American Legion, page 10 United States Department Veteran Affairs, page 27 © John Kropewnicki/Dreamstime. LLC, and page 35 © GIPhotoStock Z/Almy.

10 9 8 7 6 5 4 3 2 1

ISBN 10: 0-13-288695-2
ISBN 13: 978-0-13-288695-6

CONTENTS

Introduction

IF YOU ARE A VETERAN, active duty military, reservist/guardsman, interested family member, or just wondering about entering service to gain educational benefits, this guide is for you. Many have built on military service to find success in higher education, just as we did. You can, too, and you'll be better equipped with this information resource.

The unemployment rate in the United States is high. But the Department of Labor reports that those who have served in the military since 9/11 are even more likely to be unemployed than their civilian counterparts. Fortunately, getting your college degree can help. According to Bureau of Labor statistics, the chances of employment for those with a bachelor's degree are significantly better than for those with only a high school diploma, and better still for those with an advanced degree. A college degree also boosts your earnings potential, opening the door to higher-paying jobs.

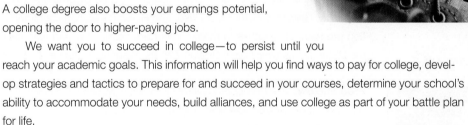

We want you to succeed in college—to persist until you reach your academic goals. This information will help you find ways to pay for college, develop strategies and tactics to prepare for and succeed in your courses, determine your school's ability to accommodate your needs, build alliances, and use college as part of your battle plan for life.

Education Web Resources

To start exploring the range of dedicated online resources for active duty military personnel and veterans interested in higher education, visit the following two portals:

- *Military OneSource (www.militaryonesource.com) offers general information, links, and articles on a wide range of military-related topics, including college.*
- *Milblogging.com (www.milblogging.com) provides a searchable index of informal commentaries.*

About the Authors

Phil McNair and Fred Stielow are dedicated military educators who work together at the online American Public University System with its flagship American Military University (AMU), the leading university for today's military. They also collaborate on post-traumatic stress disorder (PTSD) scholarship, and on the Sloan Consortium workshops "Serving Military Students" and "PTSD and Stress in the Online Classroom."

Phil McNair, retired Army colonel and Vice President for Strategic Initiatives, was a principle architect behind AMU's sector-leading military outreach program. He has also headed programs in Marketing, Student Retention, and Academic Services.

McNair served as company commander in the 25th Infantry Division (Light), assistant professor of military science at University of Texas El Paso, battalion commander in the 101st Airborne Division (Air Assault), and executive officer to the Army's Deputy Chief of Staff for Personnel. His office was at ground zero in the Pentagon on 9/11. He was awarded the Purple Heart for injuries sustained and the Soldier's Medal for heroism in rescuing others in the aftermath of the plane crash. At his retirement ceremony, Colonel McNair was presented the Army's highest decoration for military service—the Distinguished Service Medal. His service has been chronicled on television and in such books as *The Pentagon* and *Heroes of 9/11*.

A ROTC Cadet Corps Commander, he earned his bachelor's at Louisiana State University. His master's from the U.S. Naval War College is joined by graduate work at Central Michigan University, University of Texas, El Paso, and Harvard's Management and Leadership in Education program. He teaches in management and leadership and was nationally recognized by the Distance Learning Administration with the Wagner Educational Leadership Award in 2009.

Fred Stielow, Vice President/Dean of Libraries, represents the enlisted side. The son of a disabled WWII veteran, Stielow volunteered for the U.S. Army during Vietnam, serving in Germany as an NCO. With GI-Bill help, he earned a bachelor's, master's, and doctorate from Indiana University and M.L.S. from the University of Rhode Island.

Dr. Stielow worked for the New England Library Board and University of Louisiana Lafayette, where he helped organize the Archives of Acadian and Creole Folklore. He also directed the Amistad Research Center at Tulane, Reuther Labor Library at Wayne State, and New York's Mid-Hudson Public Library System. Consultancies range from Bowie State University and National Agricultural Library to New Orleans' Jazz and Heritage Festival, Vermont Folklife Center, and World Bank. He has been a professor at the University of Maryland and Catholic University and an adjunct at the Universities of Illinois, Puerto Rico, and Perugia, Italy.

In addition, Dr. Stielow has contributed to over 100 websites, over 100 scholarly articles and 11 books, including the forthcoming *Reinventing the Academic Library for the Web*. He has chaired the ALA's Web Advisory Committee and Intellectual Freedom Roundtable and sits on numerous advisory boards. Awards include a Fulbright Fellowship, Etter Prize for Creativity, Library of Congress's Jameson Fellowship, MCI Cybrarian of the Year, and Alumnus of the Year from the URI Library School.

Chapter 1
Paying for College

YOU MAY BE CONSIDERING COLLEGE COURSEWORK to help move up in grade, prepare for a civilian job, or continue your learning. Once you decide to attend college, how do you tap into government-funded tuition assistance and other educational benefits? This chapter focuses on the financial resources dedicated to military personnel and veterans.

Financial assistance depends on your military status—for instance, are you enlisted active duty military, a commissioned or non-commissioned officer, reservist/guardsman, or veteran? It also depends on your branch of service, such as the Coast Guard or Department of Defense (DoD) military—Army, Navy, Air Force, or Marines. We'll turn first to those on active duty and then look at reservists/guardsmen and veterans.

Financial Aid for Active Duty Military

For those of you on active duty—no matter what your branch of service— the DoD's **Defense Activity for Non-Traditional Education Support (DANTES)** program coordinates all forms of educational benefits for **voluntary off-duty education (VolEd)**. This differs from the training and coursework you complete on duty and under orders. As examples of VolEd, consider a Marine studying for an education degree or an Air Force pilot pursuing an MBA to prepare for life as civilians.

DANTES coordinates with the non-military sector through the **American Council on Education (ACE)** and participating **Servicemembers Opportunity Colleges (SOC)**. SOC is a consortium of "military friendly" schools across the United States. These agree to focus on the special educational needs and issues of active duty military and veterans, including transfer credits.

QUICK TERM

TA (tuition assistance): Government financial support used to pay the cost of enrolling in courses at an accredited higher education institution.

The most common type of governmental financial support for active duty military is **tuition assistance (TA)**. TA primarily serves enlisted personnel. Officers can receive TA funds under certain conditions and incur an extra service obligation for its use. Distribution of TA benefits varies slightly by branch of service, but Figure 1-1 gives a general overview of what is and is not covered and how the assistance is provided.

"A better educated soldier is a better soldier…more useful to his country and more useful to himself." General Omar Bradley

FIGURE 1-1 | **Department of Defense Tuition Assistance**

What TA Covers	• Funds to cover tuition along with computer, laboratory, and special fees up to a maximum of $250 per credit hour • Total funds limited to $4,500 per year (Oct 1–Sept. 30) (Navy limits differ.)
Which Courses Are Eligible for Assistance	• Courses must be part of an "academic degree plan" leading to a degree or certificate • Course offerings must be from a nationally or regionally accredited college
What TA Does NOT Cover	• Books • Flight training • Taking the same course twice • Continuing education units
When You Must Repay TA	• If you leave military service before the course finishes • If you fail the class • If you quit for reasons other than illness, transfer, or mission requirements
How Assistance Is Provided	• Monies are made available on a course-by-course basis • Course applications are processed and typically pre-approved through the Education Service Officer (ESO) on a military base or ship; the process is often automated

DANTES Information

DANTES' website (www.dantes.doded.mil/Dantes_homepage.html) includes information about a range of services in addition to tuition assistance. Here are some examples:

- *Facilitating examinations for high school equivalency, college admissions, college credit, and various certifications.*
- *Providing distance-learning catalogs that list courses offered by properly accredited schools.*
- *Managing the cooperating contracts with the American Council on Education (ACE) and participating Servicemembers Opportunity Colleges (SOC).*

Army: TA and Other Aid Programs

Two key resources offer help with Army TA: the Army's VolEd portal, known as GoArmyEd (www.goarmyed.com/login.aspx), and Army Education Centers. Website access to GoArmyEd requires a user name and password for full services. The site automates many manual TA processes that the Army ESO usually performs, saving valuable time.

To access the full range of TA benefits, make sure to use GoArmyEd, but also visit an Army Education Center in person and follow this recommended routine:

- Meet with a counselor to declare an educational goal, and create a plan to reach it.
- Listen carefully as the counselor explains TA procedures to you, including the requirements for TA reimbursements and, if applicable, your obligations in the program.
- Active duty servicemembers must request TA online at GoArmyEd. Your counselor can help you through the process.

You must request TA on a course-by-course basis. If you wish to take a course with a school that does not participate in the electronic GoArmyEd course schedule, complete a TA Request form at GoArmyEd that will be routed to an Army Education Counselor for review and approval.

Navy: TA and the Navy College Program

The Navy's two main support options for college financial aid are TA and a Navy college program. Both options are coordinated through the **Navy College Program (NCP)** in the Center for Personal and Professional Development (www.navycollege.navy.mil/dsp_academic.cfm).

To apply for TA funds, sailors start by contacting the NCP office. That office provides educational counseling and helps create an individual education plan, which is required before enrolling in a TA-funded course. To save time and keep costs down, the Navy recommends the following:

- Check with your Navy College office to determine if you can take a **College-Level Examination Program (CLEP)** or a DANTES Subject Standardized Test exam in place of a course requirement. If sailors pass these tests, they can earn college credit.
- Complete a TA application form—NETPDTC 1560.3 Rev. (04/04)—listing coursework and any related fees.
- Carefully read the second page of the application—the Tuition Assistance Application Agreement. Make sure to complete the requested information at the bottom of the page.
- Receive your commander's approval and signature to enroll in your courses.
- Return your TA application to your Navy College office for processing.
- Keep a copy of the TA Authorization Voucher your Navy College will prepare for you to give to the school once TA application is authorized.

Education Service Officers (ESOs) and base centers are pivotal. For locations, visit the Directory of Education Centers (www.dantes.doded.mil/Dantes_web/apps/edcenters/EdCenterSearch.aspx).

QUICK TERMS

NCP (Navy College Program): The organizational element of the Navy responsible for higher education.

CLEP (College-Level Examination Program): An assessment program that offers more than 30 subject matter tests to determine if college credit can be given to the test-taker based on test performance.

NCPACE (Navy College Program for Afloat College Education): An educational program that provides seagoing Navy members (and, in some cases, Marines) the opportunity to take tuition-free courses on ship.

AFVEC (Air Force Virtual Education Center): The online portal through which airmen apply for tuition assistance.

Hint

For more information on deployed education for Marines, see www.usmc-mccs.org/education/deployeded.cfm.

The **Navy College Program for Afloat College Education (NCPACE)** provides sea-going personnel with higher education opportunities, often through instructors who teach classes onboard. Sailors and, to a limited degree, Marines are eligible on ships with a Unit Identification Code (UIC) of type 2 or 4. NCPACE (www.navycollegepace.com) funds all tuition, but students are responsible for their textbooks and related materials. Courses are contracted with accredited Servicemembers Opportunity Colleges-Navy (SOCNAV) and subject to available berthing for resident instructors (www.navycollege.navy.mil/ncp/ncpace.cfm#o).

Marines: TA and Other Assistance

The Marine Corps prides itself on VolEd. For funding opportunities, check with the Marine installation's Lifelong Learning Center or Education Office. Alternatively, the Marine Corps Community Service (MCCS) provides a clearing house on education benefits (www.usmc-mccs.org/education/mta.cfm). You may also want to examine the SOCMAR portal (www.soc.aascu.org/socmar/Default.html) for further information.

- **Tuition Assistance (TA)** is the main financial support for Marines interested in higher education. First-time students must first complete a TA orientation class and take a Test of Adult Basic Education (TABE). Anyone scoring below 10.2 on the test must enroll in the Military Academic Skills Program (MASP) to ensure their success in the classroom.

- **Deployed Education** is a special plan to provide undergraduate courses to afloat Marines and those stationed in MCB Camp Pendleton and MCAS Cherry Point. The Corps has signed agreements with several accredited academic institutions to offer the courses. Those institutions agree to employ qualified Marines as their instructors.

- **NCPACE** from the Navy is also available to embarked, shipboard Marines on a space-available basis, but only after the Navy's 10-person minimum is met for its personnel.

Air Force: TA and Other Assistance

The Air Force offers the most automated access to higher education benefits. Airmen must create log-on credentials and apply for TA through the **Air Force Virtual Education Center (AFVEC)** in the Air Force Portal (www.my.af.mil), where they enter basic course registration information, including:

- Exact school term dates
- Course code and precise title
- Cost per semester or quarter hour

Requests are electronically forwarded to the Air Force Education Center for review. Notice is given via email through your "My AFVEC" address and is also made available through AFVEC site log-on at the nearest Air Force Education Center.

The Air Force provides several other enlisted educational opportunities besides TA, such as the following:

- **Community College of the Air Force (CCAF)** automatically enrolls enlisted personnel. CCAF (www.au.af.mil/au/ccaf/) uniquely combines on-duty education and VolEd and is the largest accredited community college in the United States. The program is aimed at improving the skills of non-commissioned officers with associate's degrees in aircraft and missile maintenance, electronics and telecommunications, allied health, logistics and resources, or public and support services.

- The **Airman Education and Commissioning Program (AECP)** program is especially for those on a military career path. Those selected for the program remain technically on active duty but are administratively assigned to an Air Force ROTC detachment. Their job is to study as a full-time college student. Airmen selected for AECP receive a tuition-and-fees scholarship capped at $15,000, with a textbook supplement of $600 per year.

Hint

For more information about non-TA Air Force benefits, see www.airforce.com/opportunities/enlisted/education/.

Coast Guard Financial Aid

The Coast Guard is the non-DoD military branch. It belongs to the Department of Homeland Security and coordinates educational operations through the Training Center Cape May (www.uscg.mil/hq/capemay/Education/ta.asp). The Coast Guard also offers a maximum of $4,500 in annual TA, with a focus at the bachelor's and associate's degrees. Officers are also eligible for TA, but at two years of additional service for every course using their TA. For additional information, visit the SOCCOAST web site (www.soc.aascu.org/soccoast/Default.html).

QUICK TERMS

CCAF (Community College of the Air Force): A federally chartered degree-granting institution that serves Air Force enlisted personnel.

AECP (Airman Education and Commissioning Program): A program that helps enlisted members of the Air Force to earn a bachelor's degree and an officer's commission.

Joint Service Programs and Financial Aid

Some military college financial aid programs cut across service lines. DANTES coordinates several of these offerings, including the Troops to Teachers program and severely injured servicemembers scholarships:

- **Troops to Teachers (TTT):** DANTES and the Department of Education co-sponsor officers and enlisted personnel looking for a second career as a teacher. TTT offers financial support toward teacher certification in exchange for a three-year teaching commitment. The program offers counseling and referral services that identify teacher certification programs and educational requirements at the individual state level. Although not an employment bureau, TTT does offer information about job prospects. For more information, visit the TTT homepage at www.dantes.doded.mil/dantes_Web/troopstoteachers/index.asp.

- **Other College Aid for Spouses:** The National Military Family Association (www.militaryfamily.org/get-info/spouse-education/) and military spouse clubs are among those offering dedicated scholarships for military spouses. Other financial aid sources include the Navy-Marine Corps Relief Society (www.nmcrs.org/), and the VADM E.P. Travers Scholarship and Loan Program, which is for spouses of active duty and retired members.

Financial Aid for National Guard and Reserves

Because of a variety of policies and resources that can differ by state and even, in some cases, by unit, it is worth checking your situation to find educational assistance that may be available to you. In some cases, members of the Army and Air Force Reserves are eligible for TA, just like their active duty counterparts. Yet, Navy and Marine Corps reservists are not eligible for TA. Fortunately, DANTES has helped simplify the search and employs a Reserve Component Advisor for added assistance (www.dantes.doded.mil/Dantes_web/rc/index.asp).

Those interested and assigned or located near a military installation should make the base education offices an early stop. Given expectations with the new GI Bill, many schools have or are adding specially trained advisors for the Guard and Reserves. Let's look at the National Guard college aid resources first and the Reserves second.

National Guard

Unless mobilized for federal service, individual states control Air and Army National Guard troops, including educational benefits. How to obtain financial aid and determine the amount provided varies from state to state. For example, some states allow National Guardsmen to attend state schools tuition-free. They may or may not also provide funding to attend privately operated schools in the state or out-of-state schools. Fortunately, the Guard has Family Assistance Centers in each state that you can locate through the Local Community Resource Finder found on the Bureau of National Guard website (www.jointservicessupport.org). These are shown in Figure 1-2.

Hint

For financial aid information for the National Guard, try www.nationalguard.com/benefits/ money-for-college.

In addition to the prospect of state-provided educational support, the Guard offers two major scholarships for full-time students. These awards pay either tuition and mandatory fees or room and board (not to exceed $10,000 per year) in addition to a monthly stipend. To apply, you must be a U.S. citizen and high school graduate with a 920 on the SAT or a 19 on the ACT. Following college graduation, cadets incur a new Military Service Obligation (MSO) of eight years of service in the Guard.

FIGURE **1-2** | **Local Community Resource Finder, Bureau of National Guard Website**

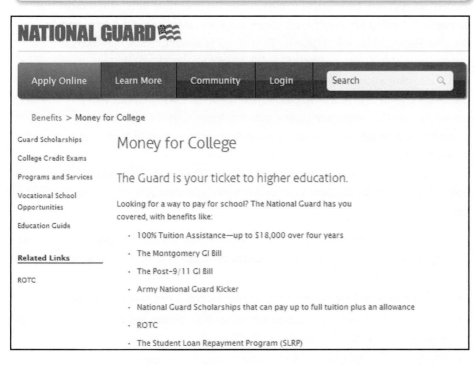

DEDNG scholarship (Dedicated Army National Guard scholarship): A scholarship for full-time students in the National Guard that covers tuition and other college expenses plus a monthly allowance.

Simultaneous Membership Program (SMP): A program through which enlisted members can participate in a ROTC program while in college and be a member of a military Guard or Reserve unit at the same time.

GRFD scholarship (Guaranteed Reserve Forces Duty scholarship): A scholarship that covers tuition, books, and a monthly stipend for full-time Juniors and Seniors in the Reserve forces in a ROTC SMP.

1. **Dedicated Army National Guard (DEDNG) Scholarship**: These scholarships cover full tuition and are available for entering freshmen. There is no limit to the number of scholarships given out each year in every state and U.S. territory. Recipients also receive up to $1,200 for books and are paid a monthly allowance in the following amounts: $350 per month during the sophomore year, $400 per month during the junior year, and $500 per month during the senior year. If you are in the **Simultaneous Membership Program (SMP)**—that is, if you participate in the Guard and your college's ROTC program at the same time—the Guard sweetens the pot with drill pay, which is equivalent to a sergeant (E-5). Graduate students can apply if they have only two years remaining until the completion of their degree.

2. **Guaranteed Reserve Forces Duty (GRFD) Scholarship**: These scholarships are similar to DEDNG scholarships. To apply, you must be entering your junior year with a GPA of 2.5 or higher and enlistment in a ROTC SMP. A GRFD scholarship brings a tuition package and $1,200 for books, as well as a ROTC allowance for 10 months of the year at $400 per month during the junior year and $500 per month during the senior year. And, as a member of the Guard, you also receive drill pay.

Reserves

Reserve members should check with their reserve unit for specific information about what financial support may be available to them. Individual units have different resources that can be helpful in funding tuition or paying off student loans. Members of the Army and Air Force Selective Reserves are often eligible for TA in amounts similar to active duty members.

Today, ROTC is growing on many college campuses. ROTC is a college elective that allows you to earn a commission straight out of college as a second lieutenant in the Army. The course consists of both academic classes and hands-on training. Check with your college to see if it has a ROTC program or cross-enrollment agreements with nearby schools. Also, plan to visit the local detachment and talk to one of the cadre members or to discuss it with a local military recruiter.

Scholarship programs are available through ROTC that can be used to pay for tuition, books, and fees. National Guard and Reservists can participate in ROTC through the SMP. In general:

- Students can participate in the initial phase, normally the first two years, without incurring a military obligation. The second phase or receipt of a ROTC scholarship mandates military service.
- Programs have at least one required summer training component off-campus.
- Campus "detachments" are staffed with active duty officers and non-commissioned officers who teach classes and prepare ROTC cadets for commissioning.
- ROTC classes often carry academic credit toward your graduation.
- Participating students can receive monthly monetary stipends after passing certain milestones.

Financial Aid for Veterans

The Veterans Administration (VA) runs two main GI Bill programs and several secondary educational benefit offerings. The same Application for VA Education Benefits (VA Form 22-1990, gibill.va.gov/documents/VA_22_1990.pdf) works for all programs and, supposedly, requires only an hour to complete. Determining which program and your entitlement(s), however, may take longer. It depends in part on when and how long you served in the military, how you were discharged, and whether you contributed to the program when on active duty. In some cases, veterans and active duty personnel can qualify for more than one program or use one to supplement another. The amounts can also vary significantly by program (gibill.va.gov/resources/benefits_resources/rate_tables.html#Ch01), and the nature of the benefits is still evolving.

Thankfully, many colleges have a trained VA funds officer to help. The American Legion's website (www.legion.gov) also holds a wealth of information—including a benefits calculator, shown in Figure 1-3.

FIGURE **1-3** | **VA Education Website Benefits Calculator**

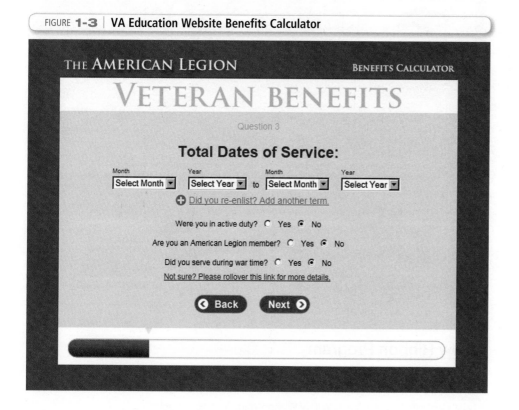

Hint

Military.com has a helpful set of tools for the GI Bill at www.military.com/Post911GiBill.

The Post-9/11 GI Bill

The Post-9/11 GI Bill, as shown in Figure 1-4, is the main source of college financial aid for most new veterans and is the most generous GI Bill since the World War II version. Eligibility is aimed at those honorably discharged after serving for at least 90 days after 9/11/2001, and benefits may transfer to dependents. The program offers as much as 36 months of educational support, including the following:

- **Tuition and Fees** The bill covers all in-state costs at a public university or up to $17,500 a year at a private institution of higher learning. More expensive private schools can offer full coverage by joining the Yellow Ribbon Program.

- **Housing Allowance** Calculated on the Basic Allowance for Housing (BAH) schedule for an E-5 with dependents. For those attending foreign universities, the rate is $1,347 per month. Students at online universities and on active duty are ineligible.

- **Books and Supplies** Prorated at $1,000 for full-time enrollment but not available for active duty personnel.

FIGURE **1-4** | **VA Education Website GI Bill**

Yellow Ribbon Program

The Yellow Ribbon Program is an element of the Post-9/11 GI Bill. It allows educational institutions to partner with the VA to provide additional funding for qualified veterans. Check your school's website to see if it is a Yellow Ribbon-participating school.

Montgomery GI Bill-Selected Reserve (MGIB-SR)

The GI Bill offers Reservists and Guardsmen—the Selected Reserve—up to 36 months of benefits while on non-regular service or after discharge for the total number of months mobilized plus four months. Your unit is responsible to code eligibility and give you the enabling DD Form

2384-1. In addition, you must have your high school degree or equivalent, finish your initial active duty for training, and be in good standing in an active Selected Reserve unit with a six-year service obligation. Officers must agree to an additional six years.

Other Aid Programs

The VA offers several other college assistance programs, including:

- **GI Bill Buy-Up Program:** This program allows those on active duty to make contributions to increase benefit payouts. Every $20 that you put in before separation returns $180. If you contribute the maximum ($600), you gain an additional $150 per month for a total of $5,400 over the total 36 months of entitlement. To be eligible, you must be on active duty; have joined the service after June 30, 1985; and not be a veteran using the Post-9/11 GI Bill.

- **Reserve Educational Assistance Program (REAP):** This program provides educational assistance to those in the Selected Reserve who were called to at least 90 days of active duty for authorized Contingency Operations, such as Afghanistan and Iraq.

- **National Call to Service Program (NCS):** This DoD program, administered by the VA, requires a three-level commitment: 15 months of active duty in a designated occupation specialty after initial training, then up to 24 months in the Selected Reserve, and a final obligation in the Reserves, AmeriCorps, or other designated domestic national service programs. NCS participation may limit eligibility in other educational programs, but it comes with an array of incentives, including a cash bonus, student loan repayment (currently up to $18,000), a monthly allowance, and coordination of benefits with the Montgomery GI Bill.

> **MGIB-AD and VEAP**
>
> *Two additional programs offer college financial aid for some veterans:*
>
> - *Montgomery GI Bill-Active Duty (MGIB-AD): The filler GI Bill between the Vietnam and post-9/11 versions, also known as Title 30, offers up to 36 months of benefits but is focused primarily on those entering service between 1985 and 1997.*
> - *Veterans Educational Assistance Program (VEAP): This innovative $2 to $1 contribution match for educational funds is limited to those who entered the service between January 1, 1977, and June 30, 1985.*

Concluding Thoughts

You've now explored the main financial resources for active duty, reserves, and veterans as of early 2012. As with any government benefit, these may change. Make sure to check the listed websites and, especially, the base educational offices. In addition, don't forget to make use of your university's financial aid offices and conduct searches for non-military support. Remember, too, to fill out a Free Application for Federal Student Aid (FAFSA) each year—the sooner, the better.

Financial Aid opportunities for military and veteran students are often available through the goodwill and generosity of non-profit organizations, clubs, churches, and support groups. It makes good sense to do a thorough check via the Internet, your base education center, your school's veteran's center, and by asking for information from local agencies and organizations. You might be eligible for money that's specific to your community, your degree program, or even your school. You have nothing to lose by seeking all possible funding sources!

Chapter 2
Preparing for College Success

WHETHER THIS IS YOUR FIRST OR FIFTH TIME selecting a school, four steps pave the way as you prepare for success in college.

First, evaluate how well the college suits your academic and personal needs, including how military friendly it is. Second, find ways to earn course credits based on your military and life experience. Third, take stock of your basic skills, such as math and writing, and the military skills that may give you a strategic advantage. Finally, set specific academic goals as part of your graduation campaign.

Evaluating Your School Choice

Because your needs differ from those of other students, it's worth taking the time to evaluate your choice of school by considering questions such as these:

- Does the college have the right community of students for me?
- Does the type of college suit my needs?
- Is the college accredited?
- Does the college offer the courses and degrees I want?
- Is the school military friendly?

Finding answers to these questions can help you avoid costly mistakes, such as choosing a school that is unaccredited or will not award college credit for applicable service training.

Student Community

Unlike the majority of **traditional students** who attend college shortly after high school graduation and are living on their own for the first time, you are the epitome of a **non-traditional student**. You took time off between high school and college—or maybe during college—to engage in other activities, such as work or military service. You've lived on your own without parental support and have experienced challenges that few others will. For some, you may have faced life-and-death situations. If you're active duty military, chances are that you've moved or changed schedules due to your service

obligations. If you're a veteran, you're likely to be coping with financial and family responsibilities that may limit your flexibility, slow the pace of your education to part-time status, or even interrupt your education altogether.

Find out if the college has a significant number of other non-traditional students (the admissions or registrar's office can often provide statistics on student population). Even better, find out if the college has other veterans or active duty military and what services the college offers in support. Having fellow students who understand your background and experience can make a huge difference. If the college does not have these kinds of students, consider your social life and the prospects for finding enough people to connect with. You may want to avoid an isolating, "fish-out-of-water" experience. If you are married, don't forget to consider your family's needs as well.

Type of School

Another key factor to evaluate is what type of school fits your needs best. Options range from traditional brick-and-mortar universities to fully online institutions that you attend virtually:

- **Residential School:** On a residential college campus, you may be able to attend part-time, but full-time enrollment is more common. For students considering residential private and selective state schools, entry can be competitive and costs may be high, but the prestige is often enticing.

  Your experiences at a residential school will depend on the size of the campus, where it's located, and the college culture. Is it a hard "study" school, a party school, or a combination? Is it a huge school in a metropolitan area with Division I sports, or is it a small, rural liberal arts college that only offers intramural activities? Above all, make sure you (and, perhaps, your family) feel comfortable in your environment.

- **Commuting School:** A school where students do not live on campus, such as community colleges, is often the most practical for returning veterans, especially those with families and/or those in need of supplemental employment. Commuting schools may also be available through programs on base for active duty military. Entry is typically not competitive, part-time enrollment is common, and costs are usually much more affordable than those for residential schools. Trade-offs include the loss of a campus residential lifestyle and attending an institution with less prestige. With two-year commuting schools, another disadvantage is the effort it takes to transfer to a four-year school and the potential loss of credits. However, many two-year commuter schools have "articulation" agreements with in-state, four-year schools or other institutions to ensure credits transfer easily.

- **Online College or University:** Online education has become the top choice for active duty military. The online option is highly attractive to veterans who have difficult job schedules or need time to transition and adjust to civilian life.

  Most colleges and universities now offer some type of online coursework, but the true online college or university is quite different. Rather than set meeting times in a lecture hall, learning typically takes place on the computer when it's convenient for you. Rather than Fall, Spring, and Summer

QUICK TERMS

Residential school: A college or university where students normally live on or near campus while attending school.

Commuting school: A college or university where students typically commute to campus.

Online college or university: A higher education institution whose curriculum consists of only online courses.

Hint

Active duty military may want to consider steps for establishing a home state based on a desirable state university before discharge.

sessions with set classroom hours, you may find monthly starts and classrooms open 24/7. Admittance is typically easy and rolling—it can often happen any time of the year. Despite these advantages, however, online education is not for everyone. It requires self-discipline, an ability to work on one's own, and strong reading and writing skills. Instead of listening to lectures and talking in class, expect heavy reading loads and an emphasis on written "discussion."

Given the newness of the online sector and the potential for misuse, thoroughly evaluate any college of this type. Avoid brokers, who may advertise on television or in pop-up ads on your computer screen. Instead, spend time on the school's website. Check log-in requirements and accreditation status carefully. Costs for tuition and course materials will vary greatly and fee policies can be confusing, so make certain you read—and understand—the fine print.

Accreditation

Accreditation is a crucial factor for evaluating a college. The process engages a higher education institution in a evaluation to meet educational standards in compliance with the Council for Higher Education Accreditation and the Department of Education. Students who do not attend an accredited school, or who attend a school that doesn't have proper accreditation, run several risks. For instance, degrees from schools without sufficient accreditation can harm you during the job search process. Also, hard-earned credit hours may not transfer to schools with proper accreditation.

To qualify for tuition assistance, the institution you attend must be at least nationally accredited. Figure 2-1 reviews and describes the three main types of accreditation.

Course Offerings/Scheduling

Spend time with course listings to see whether the classes you're interested in are offered, what the prerequisites are (if any), how often the courses you need to complete your degree or certificate are offered, and whether the course times work with your schedule.

Some schools offer a wide range of courses but may not have the staff or student interest to support the field of emphasis you want to pursue. Investigate and ask questions. For instance, some colleges only offer key classes once per year, which can make getting into those courses extremely difficult. Find students in the field you're interested in, and ask them how easy it is to get into and take the courses you'll need.

QUICK TERM

Accreditation: a formal evaluation of a higher education institution to see if it meets the standards of an accrediting agency.

FIGURE **2-1** | **Understanding Types of Accreditation**

Type	Description	Key Examples
National accreditation	• The minimum standard of accreditation • Satisfies tuition assistance accreditation requirements	• Accrediting Council for Independent Colleges and Schools • Accrediting Commission for Career Schools and Colleges of Technology • Distance Education Training Council (the major agency)
Regional accreditation	• The highest standard of accreditation for a college • Satisfies tuition assistance requirements	• Middle States Association of Colleges and Schools • New England Association of Schools and Colleges • North Central Association of Colleges and Schools • Northwest Commission on Colleges and Universities • Southern Association of Colleges and Schools • Western Association of Colleges and Schools
Specialized accreditation	• Additional accreditation specific to disciplines or professions, especially those requiring licenses • Normally supplements the institution's overall accreditation to show how individual degree programs meet the highest standards	• NCATE: The National Council for Accreditation of Teacher Education (accredits education degree programs) • AACSB: The Association to Advance College Schools of Business (accredits business degree programs)

Military Friendly Schools

Government programs can help you learn more about schools that claim to be military friendly. One key program, known as **Servicemembers Opportunity Colleges (SOC)**, operates through a contract between Defense Activity for Non-Traditional Education Support (DANTES) and the American Association of State Colleges and Universities (AASCU). Originally, its main objective was to solve problems with credit transfer for frequently deployed U.S. military personnel. Today, the SOC (www.soc.aascu.org/socconsortium/Default.html) serves as a cooperative of some 1,900 accredited colleges and universities and works in conjunction with 15 higher education associations and the DoD to serve military students effectively.

These self-pronounced military friendly schools provide associate's, bachelor's, and master's degrees for military students and their adult dependent family members. More specifically, these schools agree to offer the following:

1. **Reasonable Transfer of Credit** Students avoid excessive loss of previously earned credits from other schools.

2. **Reduced Academic Residency** To accommodate the mobility of those in the military, students can graduate from an institution even if they do not have a final year or term in residence.

3. **Credit for Military Training and Experience** These schools agree to use the American Council of Education (ACE) *Guide to the Evaluation of Educational Experiences in the Armed Services* (militaryguides.acenet.edu/) in determining academic credit for military training and experience.

4. **Credit for Nationally Recognized Testing Programs** SOC member schools award credit for at least one nationally recognized testing program, such as the College-Level Examination Program (CLEP) or the Excelsior College Examinations (ECE).

Choosing an SOC school affords many other benefits, such as clear and accurate information about financial obligations, student loans, scholarships, and drop/add policies. If you aren't at an SOC school, compare your school to SOC policies in the areas of credit, residency, accreditation, enrollment, course information, support services, and the other safeguards mentioned in Figure 2-2.

FIGURE **2-2** | **Five Samples from the SOC Military Student Bill of Rights**

Military students attending SOC member schools have the right to...

- Accurate information about a school's programs, requirements, and accreditation.
- A clear, complete explanation of enrollment procedures and all resulting financial obligations. No high-pressure enrollment procedures are allowed.
- Appropriate academic screening and course placement based on student readiness.
- Appropriate, accessible academic and student support services.
- Clearly stated procedures about the effect of military duties, such as mobilization, activation, and temporary duty assignments, on academic standing and financial responsibilities.

Although you may attend more than one institution, each decision is major—especially in terms of the institution that will grant your degree. Do some comparison shopping, and use the checklist in Figure 2-3 as a guide to help you make more informed decisions about how well your school meets your needs.

FIGURE **2-3** | **Preliminary Evaluation Checklist**

College:_____ Contact(s):_____	
Factor	**Rating/Comments**
1 What type of school: ☐ Resident ☐ Commuter ☐ Online	
2 Accreditation: ☐ National ☐ Regional ☐ Special ☐ None	
3 Meets my program/degree needs: ☐ Yes ☐ No ☐ Unsure	
4 Credit Hour Cost: $_____	
5 Extra Fees: $_____	
6 Books/Course Materials (estimate): $_____	
7 Course Scheduling: ☐ Fine ☐ Problems ☐ Unsure	
8 Military Friendly: ☐ Yes ☐ No ☐ Unsure	
9 Transfer Credit/Credit for Military Experience/PLA: ☐ Good ☐ Poor ☐ Unsure	
10 Transportation/Parking: ☐ Good ☐ Poor ☐ Unsure ☐ N/A	
11 Library/Research Services: ☐ Good ☐ Poor ☐ Unsure	
12 Tutorial Support: ☐ Good ☐ Poor ☐ Unsure	
13 Other Support (mental, physical) : ☐ Good ☐ Poor ☐ Unsure	
14 Sports/Activities: ☐ Good ☐ Bad ☐ Unsure ☐ N/A	
15 Community/Family Factors: ☐ Good ☐ Poor ☐ Unsure	

Getting Credit for Military Experience

Many colleges offer course credit hours for military training courses or allow you to petition for credit based on what you have learned through life experience. Any credit you get outside the classroom can shorten the amount of time it takes to obtain your degree and lessen the amount of money you will need.

One key to gaining credit for your military experience is to work closely with your school's transfer credit department to ensure that you get all the credit to which you are entitled. Nothing is simple, however. Military students often earn a significant amount of credit over time and find they still have a long way to go to obtain a degree. Your advisor, transfer credit counselor, or Education Service Officer (ESO) should be able to explain how you can get the maximum amount of credit and how to use that credit most effectively in gaining your degree.

> **Hint**
>
> *Just because you receive credit for something does not mean that particular credit will apply to your degree.*

ACE Recommendations

The American Council on Education (ACE) provides recommendations for the amount of college credits students can earn for military training programs. If your school accepts the ACE recommendations, you may start college with several credit hours. Even if your school doesn't follow the ACE recommendations, however, you may be able to petition for credit by citing the guidelines.

> **ACE Guide Online**
>
> *The ACE Guide to the Evaluation of Educational Experiences in the Armed Services (militaryguides. acenet.edu/) is the standard reference work for analyzing military training and experiences for the award of college credits.*

CLEP

Administered through the College Board, the CLEP college-level examinations test a student's knowledge in specific academic areas. If you pass a CLEP test, your school may give you credit for a comparable class. In some cases, your military base education center can administer CLEP tests. Although there is a fee to take the tests (some, but not all, military programs cover the cost of this test), the fee is certainly much less than paying to take a college class. To learn more about CLEP tests, visit the College Board website (clep.collegeboard.org).

DANTES Standardized Tests

DANTES offers standardized tests, called **DANTES Standardized Subject-Matter Tests (DSSTs)**, specifically for military personnel and eligible civilians. Unlike CLEP tests, which are focused solely on lower-level college credit, DSSTs cover many different levels and subjects. In fact, DANTES offers tests for more than 35 different subjects, ranging from technical writing to ethics to algebra. ACE recommends three hours of credit for each test. Learn more at the DANTES website (www.dantes.doded.mil/DANTES_WEB/ EXAMINATIONS/DSST.HTM).

> **QUICK TERM**
>
> **DSSTs** (DANTES Standardized Subject-Matter Tests): Standardized tests offered through DANTES to obtain college-level credit if the test-taker obtains a passing score.

AARTS, SMARTS, and Other Military Transcripts

To obtain credit for your military experience, you will need a copy of your military education record so that college or university officials can evaluate what you have done and your eligibility for academic credit. Online access is often the simplest, fastest way to obtain transcripts:

1. **Army/Navy/Marine Corps** ACE helps maintain the records database for the Army at the Army/American Council on Education Registry Transcript System (aarts.army.mil), or AARTS, and for the Navy and Marine Corps at smart.navy.mil/smart/welcome.do.

2. **Air Force** If you're in the Air Force, visit the Community College of the Air Force site at www.au.af.mil/au/ccaf/transcripts.asp.

3. **Coast Guard** For copies of Coast Guard transcripts, visit www.uscg.mil/hq/cgi/active_duty/go_to_college/official_transcript.asp.

Prior Learning Assessments

Your school may also evaluate skills from non-traditional learning for course credit. Prior learning assessment (PLA) programs take many forms, but they generally require you to provide evidence that you have mastered the learning objectives that map to particular college courses or degree programs. Ask about PLA at your school to see what is available and how it works. Make sure the credit you seek actually applies towards your degree, and don't expect it to transfer to another school without a separate review.

Refresher Topics

Similar to basic training, it will help if you are "in shape" when it comes to your education. Non-traditional students are often intimidated by two basic skills—writing and math. Our advice is to dive in, but don't hesitate to use your school's facilities. Visit the library, take self-paced labs and tutorials, or go to individual tutoring sessions. If you're active duty or a military dependent, the DoD has also contracted for unlimited individual tutoring hours with Tutor.Com (www.tutor.com/military).

Writing

From our experience, the writing skills that you developed in the military can be honed to fit academic requirements, but be prepared to change. Military reports, official correspondence, or letters home are not the same as a student research paper, interpretive essay, book review, or lab report—each of which has its own requirements and expectations. College papers are also distinguished by two elements that may require a bit of mastery.

- **Style Guides:** Each academic discipline has a formal set of rules for writing, layout, grammar, and manner of citation. To meet instructor expectations, make sure you know which one is in use for each course—and follow it. The two major guides are *Publication Manual of the American Psychological Association* (APA) and the *Chicago Manual of Style* (also known as Turabian), but you could encounter a slew of others—American Medical Association (AMA), Bluebook, and Modern Language Association (MLA).

- **Research and Peer-Reviewed Literature:** Your instructors will likely demand scholarly or "peer-reviewed" materials in your research papers and essays. Unlike Wikipedia and most Google searches through open Web resources, scholarly materials have passed a rigorous review by other experts in

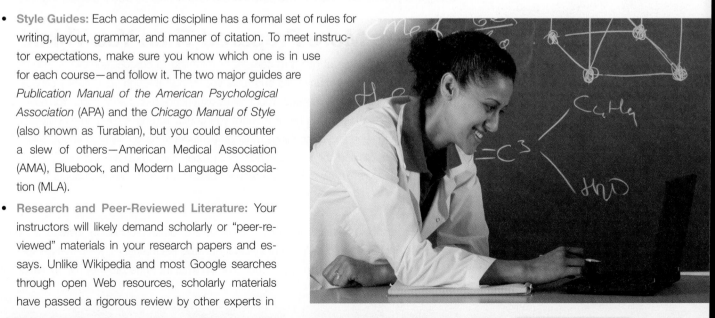

the field. They are often in the "Deep Web"—licensed materials that the college pays for. To access these materials, you usually need to visit the library in person or online.

Hint

Review scholarly journals in the field to see how those authors approach writing and research citations.

Approach each writing assignment as if it were a task assigned to you by your commander. Follow the instructor's directions for formatting as carefully as you would follow other orders. Give thought to what you want to say, write carefully, and avoid slang and "texting" language. Proofread your papers after you've used your word processing software's spelling/grammar checking tools. Students typically lose most of their points through carelessness and inattention to detail, two deficits that should not apply to you.

Above all, cite. The Web makes it all too easy to inadvertently plagiarize. Cite sources for direct quotations, when paraphrasing, with visuals or music, or if you use an idea from someone else's work.

> **Wikipedia Alert**
>
> *Wikipedia is an excellent source for launching research projects, but it can get you into trouble. Use Wikipedia for background to help frame your knowledge, and mine the citations at the end of its articles to begin your research. However, don't quote or cite it. Style rules, whatever the manual, uniformly recommend against citing any encyclopedia.*

Math

Many students fear taking math or math-related classes, such as engineering or statistics. In the military, unless you were in an engineering or finance specialty, you probably weren't required to do a lot of math. Before taking a course, or even entrance exams or assessments, it may be wise to do some preparatory work. To refresh your skills, consider using SAT, ACT, or other test preparation books, online sites, or prep courses. You can enhance your skills and reduce anxiety in the process. Higher education publishers also have online math programs to work through and assess any holes you need to work on.

Once in class, step up. Ask questions, and find help—immediately—if you need it. Math-related courses and subjects like languages are linear, so it is very hard to catch up if you miss a building block or are confused by a concept. Math tutoring sites are available online for self-study, and your college should have personalized tutorial help outside the classroom.

You Are More Prepared Than You Think!

You might find the idea of going to college, or returning to college, somewhat intimidating. Recognize, though, that many skills and traits you've built through your military service have prepared you for success in college. Your military experience has changed you. You have probably accomplished things you never thought you could. You have overcome obstacles, met challenges, and seen and done things most other students have only read about. Take stock of your current skills and abilities to see how well-prepared you really are. Let's look at three key ways in which you are likely to be more prepared than traditional college students.

Maturity

While college should be taken seriously, it is not a life-or-death proposition. Instead, it is a tool you use to get the job done. Most military students have the maturity to keep that perspective. They approach it with a determined attitude to learn what they need so they can move forward with their life goals.

As part of that maturity, you have learned to get help when you need it. You may not be an expert writer, but you can develop a strategy and find the allies and resources you need to write a complicated research paper. If you need help in a tough class, you can go get it. Treat college like any other challenge, and show the world what you can do.

Leadership

Chances are you have had some military experience leading teams or working as part of a group to accomplish a common goal. Those skills can serve you well in college, where group projects are often part of the classroom requirements. Participate in activities, and show your instructor that you are an engaged student. You might even consider running for an elected office in the student government or a club or organization. The more engaged you are, the more fun you will have and the better you will be as a student.

Planning and Time Management

To accomplish a mission in the military, detailed planning is required, which includes how resources (including time) will be used most effectively. Your planning expertise and discipline to carry out those plans in pursuit of your objectives are skills that can help you succeed as a student. Lay out your schedule as if you were planning a military operation. Determine when you will read and do your coursework, when you will take care of personal business, and when you will spend time with family and friends. Although you certainly don't want to be too rigid with your life, writing things down can help you spot trouble and time-wasters early.

Goal Setting

Now that you've prepared by evaluating your school choice, gotten credit where possible, and taken stock of your skills and abilities that need work or will help you—set clear academic goals to make sure you accomplish your mission. In the military, the road map to success is well-defined. Government regulations, policies, and procedures clearly establish criteria for promotion and advancement. Outside the military, however, *you* determine what success looks like. And to stay motivated, you need to know *why* you're in college and *how* your academic work supports your life goals. Effective goal-setting keeps you focused on your objective even when the battle to balance school and life gets tough.

Start the goal-setting process by asking yourself *why* you are going to college:

- To obtain a degree in the field you always dreamed of pursuing?
- To set an example for your children or family?
- To prepare for a new career or advance in your present career?

Once you have determined why you want to attend college, write down your goals in specific, realistic terms, and keep them in mind when the going gets tough. The most effective goals include what your aim is, how you'll reach it, and when you intend to accomplish it. Here's one example:

> To provide for my family and obtain work in a field that interests me ("why"), my goal is to graduate with a degree in optical engineering ("what") after completing 18 additional credit hours in my major ("how") within the next year-and-a-half ("when").

Post your goals where you can see them—on the refrigerator, your computer's opening screen, or your bathroom mirror. Tell family and friends about your goals so that they can give you support and nudge you when you need it. There will be times when you feel less than enthusiastic about spending time reading and doing schoolwork, and your goals can help you persist to the end. Consider each completed class as winning a small battle in your overall campaign.

We've reviewed four steps you can take to prepare for college success: evaluate how well your school meets your needs, get ahead by getting as much credit as possible, take stock of the skills you need to refresh and the skills that will help you succeed, and set clear academic goals. The work you do now to prepare can keep you motivated and save you time and money throughout your college career.

Chapter 3
The Art of Classroom Tactics

"THE GENERAL WHO WINS A BATTLE MAKES MANY CALCULATIONS in his temple before the battle is fought. The general who loses a battle makes but few calculations beforehand. Thus do many calculations lead to victory and few calculations to defeat." —Sun Tzu

Sun Tzu's observations in the *Art of War* ring true for your educational campaign and the battle to succeed in each course. In this chapter, we consider classroom tactics to support your college success: understand the aims of each course, meet instructor expectations, do more than the minimum, network, adjust your communication to suit your audience, and be prepared to manage conflicts between military duty and coursework.

Understand the Mission

Military experience teaches you the importance of a clearly defined and understood mission. Similarly, you need to know the aims for each class and how you will be evaluated. That knowledge helps you effectively plan your schedule (how you will use your time) and the use of available resources, such as the Web, textbooks, the library.

Your higher education terrain is increasingly driven toward "assessment" and measurable outcomes. Usually, the syllabus will specify course outcomes and the methods your instructor will use to assess your progress towards those outcomes with tests, assignments, projects, and class participation. To map out a winning plan in each of your courses, start with these three key elements in the syllabus:

1. **Learning Objectives:** These objectives detail what knowledge, skills, and scholarly methods you are supposed to learn in the course. Specific objectives may be tied to class sessions and assignments. Most assessments are tied to learning objectives as well.

2. **Measurement Standards:** These standards indicate the criteria or "**rubric**" that your instructor will use to grade you—for example, grammar, content, format, and accuracy—as well as how many points each can earn for meeting the criteria.

3. **Dates:** Knowing the dates of each project, assignment, and test ensures that your plan will include accurate time frames for study and preparation.

QUICK TERM

Rubric: A set of defined criteria with a specified scoring scale used to assess performance.

Follow Orders

You were trained to follow orders, so this suggestion should be simple to implement. Not unlike getting ready for an inspection, attention to detail is vital. Read the directions for tests, papers, projects, and homework. Following them prevents you from losing points that are relatively easy to earn. It also signals respect for the instructor and the learning process. Assume that your instructor (commanding officer) has reasons for taking the time to tell you what to do. Directions pertaining to fonts, margins, title page requirements, and citations are for real. And for any assignment, *turn it in on time!*

Overrun the Objective

No army ever "took the hill" by running up and stopping at the top. It charges up the hill, sweeps across the crest, and heads down the other side to completely accomplish its objective. Likewise, you can help ensure success in the classroom by going beyond what is required.

Overrunning the objective helps you become a better student and demonstrates your commitment to learning. As a bonus, committed students also get the benefit of the doubt when grades are given. Imagine how boring it must be for your instructors to read a batch of mediocre student research papers. Now, imagine what it must be like to read a well-organized student paper free of spelling and grammatical errors that also includes a few extra sources and reads fluently.

What are some ways you can overrun your course objective?

1. **Actively participate in classroom discussions** (whether face-to-face or online).

2. **Establish contact with the instructor outside the classroom.** Send an e-mail asking a question, or meet during office hours. It helps when your instructor knows who you are.

3. **Turn in your assignments early whenever possible.** Your instructor will appreciate having extra grading time, and you will signal that you care about the course-work.

4. **Overprepare.** Do the assigned reading, homework problems, labs, and so on before class discussion. If writing a paper, use more sources than required. Introduce outside (but related) information during discussions. This shows you are interested in the class topic and not merely doing the minimum for a grade.

> *Be careful! Writing more to impress can backfire unless you stay within assigned page limits. Focus on quality, not quantity.*

Understand Instructor Expectations

A key objective should be to understand what your instructor expects of you. Four tips can help:

1. *Read the course syllabus carefully to find out about the instructor's policies, grading scale, assignments, and due dates.*
2. *Ask questions if something is not totally clear.*
3. *In a course with written work, request sample papers to look at format and style.*
4. *Review the instructor's grading "rubric" for each assignment, if available.*

Coordinate with Allies

Find out if other military students are in your class, or find others who have taken the class previously. Then, network with them to gather all the useful information you can about the class requirements and your instructor—such as his or her likes and dislikes, how grades are determined, specific areas of interest, and so on. Share notes, form a study group, or try to get other military students to work with you on group projects. Visit the campus Veterans Center, and talk to vets who may have helpful information about the class or the topic. Do not go so far as to cheat by purchasing a paper or a test from someone else, but realize that there are others just like you in school and, together, you can be stronger than you will be working on your own.

Adjust Your Communication: Rank and Acronyms

The military has formal customs and a language all its own. In college, you'll need to adjust your communication to suit your audience. For instance, in the military, your rank is (or was) your identity. You were (or are) "Sergeant Jones," "Lieutenant Smith," "Petty Officer Johnson." or "Gunnery Sergeant Doe." In class at a civilian college, however, you are simply a student with no more rights and privileges than any other student. Instructors will likely call you "Mr." or "Ms." or by your first name. Even if you wear a uniform, they may not be able to understand the decorations or your hard-earned rank. Do not be offended. The instructor is your commanding officer but, as your authors will attest, far less likely to be insulting.

Is it wrong to use your rank in class or when referring to yourself in a discussion or a paper? If you are serving on active duty, you may certainly call yourself by your military rank, especially if you attend class in uniform. If you are a retiree, you have earned the right to use your retired rank, and many do, especially in correspondence. If you are a veteran, it may be appropriate in some situations to mention your military service and rank, particularly when you want to connect with other military students. Above all, however, do *not* try to use your rank to influence a classroom situation. That would likely turn the instructor and, possibly, other students against you.

Likewise, avoid using military acronyms. Even inside the military, acronyms can be confusing from one branch of the service to another. If you must use them, explain their meaning so that others can understand. Remember that in a college environment, it's best to express yourself using civilian language and terminology.

Deployments and Other Military Activities

We hope that you will be able to complete each of your courses without experiencing a military activity that impedes your ability to attend class or finish your assignments on time. However, military students do have responsibilities that can compete with classroom responsibilities. So, what is the best way to handle such a problem if it arises?

1. If you are aware of a situation that could potentially affect your ability to complete a course, you may want to adjust your course schedule to avoid problems up front. Registering for a class knowing that you are due for a deployment to the Middle East is likely not a good idea, for example, unless you are certain that you can get the work done while you are deployed.

2. Learn the dates for withdrawing from class without a penalty.

3. Keep your instructor informed about any issues that could interfere with your classroom attendance or performance. For instance, most instructors dislike being told after the fact that you missed three weeks because you were off on a training exercise. They may or may not be sympathetic enough to allow you to make up the work that you missed.

4. As soon as you have information about a schedule conflict, tell your instructor, and request an extension of time to complete your assignments or alternative ways to meet the class requirements.

Be aware that some schools are more lenient about leave than others. Also, many instructors require documentation of the conflicting military activity, such as a copy of your orders or a letter from your commander, so be prepared to furnish it.

In summary, a successful military campaign depends on thorough preparation and solid intelligence, followed by proper execution. A successful academic "campaign" is no different. Prepare yourself for class, gather intelligence from the course syllabus and other sources (like fellow students), and follow through by doing what is required in a mature, effective manner. Go after your degree with the same enthusiasm as you've pursued your military duties, and you'll be surprised by how well you will do.

Chapter 4
Military Student Resources

COLLEGE RESOURCES TO AID VETERANS and other military students can make a huge difference. The trick is to know where to look for the help you need, what to expect once you find it, and then to actually use the help. This chapter spotlights three types of resources: formal academic advising; special services for military with physical, cognitive, or medical challenges; and social resources.

Advising Services

Figuring out the intricacies of earning a college degree or certificate can be tough for any student. What courses should you take, and in what order? What do you do if you get in trouble academically, need assistance with credit transfer issues, or need advice when deciding on a major? The school will have a catalog and website to help, but the key answer is likely to turn to advisors.

Academic Advisors

Schools typically assign each student a faculty advisor on entry and/or after declaring a major or certification program. You may also have the opportunity to "adopt" or be adopted by a faculty mentor. Whether formal or informal, the faculty advisor can be the single most important factor in determining your success in college.

To find an informal advisor with a military background, consider faculty who are veterans or members of the National Guard or Reserves. Faculty with a military background often feel a special connection with hard-working military students. They are also more likely to understand your challenges and the resources that can help, including information about people with expertise in specific areas, which offices are best for which service, and so on. To find instructors with a military background, ask other military students or friends from the Veterans Center, visit the school's website for biographical information, or even visit "rate-your-instructor" sites.

Staff Counselors and Advisors

In addition to, or instead of, a formally assigned faculty advisor, your school may have counselors or non-faculty support staff advisors. Their job is to help all students, but some may be specially tasked for military and veteran students.

Academic Academic support specialists play a crucial role in many schools—especially the online universities. Staff academic advisors offer a vital path through what can be a complex and frustrating bureaucracy.

Financial If you need help accessing tuition funds, collecting benefits, or paying your tuition and fees, contact the bursar's or registrar's office. These offices often have a general finance specialist trained to help military students. In addition, schools that accept money from the Veterans Administration (VA), such as for GI Bill payments, must have a VA Certifying Official on their staff. That official is usually an excellent resource. If you cannot find a financial advisor with expertise in military financial issues, ask about finance advisors who have worked with other military students.

What to Discuss with Your Academic Advisor

1. Let your advisors know if you anticipate a deployment, lengthy training exercise, or other activity that could interfere with your schedule. Tell them as early as possible.
2. Confer about your academic goals and how you plan to accomplish them.
3. Get assistance designing a degree plan and a course schedule that meet your needs.
4. Review credit transfer, credit requirements, and the effect of both on your degree.

WORK STUDY

GRANTS

SCHOLARSHIPS

LOANS

Hint

If you have a problem that is not formally documented or you want to keep private, you may still want to talk to your instructor about informal accommodations.

Disability and Mental Health Resources

If you are disabled or impaired and need special accommodations to learn course material or participate in class effectively, help is available. Contact the Disability Support Services (DSS) office to self-identify your physical, sensory, mental, or cognitive disability. You will need to formally document the disability, and you may also need to provide up-to-date testing on how your impairment interferes with your learning. Schools that receive federal support for student loans or grants (and most of them do) are obligated to provide "reasonable" access to students with disabilities and impairments. As an example, the school may provide assistive technology, such as an automated text reader application, to a student with impaired vision.

> ### Wounded Warrior Project
> The Wounded Warrior Project (www.woundedwarriorproject.org) address the special academic and social challenges of Purple Heart recipients. Its Campus Services team works directly with your educational institution but can also provide informal mentors and an avenue for discussions. Contact them through campusservices@woundedwarriorproject.org.

QUICK TERM

Post-traumatic stress disorder (PTSD): a complex condition of persistent mental and emotional stress as the result of a terrifying event or injury.

Documented Disabilities

As mentioned, the first step in getting resources is to contact the school's DSS office to provide official documentation about your disability. That information is confidential: By law, it can only be provided to the people who need to know it to ensure you get the help you require. Once the disability is verified, the school disability official or registrar issues a letter detailing your accessibility requirements and/or special accommodations. For instance, if you have dysgraphia (a condition in which the student cannot write effectively), you may need a note taker or extra time to complete assignments or tests. However, you will need to work with each instructor to determine what accommodations apply to the specific course.

Post-Traumatic Stress Disorder

Post-Traumatic Stress Disorder (PTSD) is a complex condition of persistent mental and emotional stress as the result of a terrifying event or injury. Symptoms include the following:

- Reliving the event through flashbacks or dreams.
- Avoiding people or situations that might recall the trauma.
- Isolation.
- Decreased responsiveness ("numbing").
- Heightened stress reactions, such as startling easily or hypervigilance.

Although support is available, many military members and veterans with PTSD may not report it. Either they do not want to admit to having a mental disorder, or because they believe the information may negatively affect their careers and security clearances. If you have PTSD, we strongly urge you to consider professional help. Even if you do not want to alert your instructor, recognize that your symptoms may affect your classwork and relations with other students—and your family at home.

> **Online Option for Students with PTSD**
>
> *Do you feel stressed being in a classroom or on campus with non-veterans who may not fully understand what you went through in combat? Consider taking classes online. That environment allows you to participate in classroom activities from the comfort and security of your own space. Later, when you feel more comfortable with the transition from military life, you may opt for a physical classroom setting.*

Traumatic Brain Injury

Traumatic brain injury (TBI) occurs when a force traumatizes the brain, resulting in loss of consciousness, altered mental state, and/or a loss of memory about the event. Examples of external force include a bullet, shrapnel, or sudden acceleration or deceleration, such as a fall from a blast explosion. TBI can range from severe to mild. Mild TBI is considered to be a "signature" injury of the wars in Iraq and Afghanistan. As with PTSD, many of those with TBI do not report it or are unaware of their condition, so they fail to seek and secure help.

Symptoms of TBI vary, but they can include increased irritability, memory issues, difficulty with planning and judgment, decreased attention and concentration, and reading/auditory comprehension problems—all of which can impede learning. Accommodations for students with TBI are wide-ranging but may include assistive technologies to aid in organization or memory, assistance with note taking, test taking in a solitary environment, and so on.

Unless your condition is officially documented, the college is not required to provide accommodations, but an instructor may be willing to help without documentation. Try requesting assistive technologies, such as text or online reminders of key dates. Outside class, it can also be helpful to share your experiences and concerns with others who understand what you are going through. Campus Veterans Centers often have support groups for military students with PTSD, TBI, or combat-related issues, and many schools have Counseling or Mental Health Centers that can provide helpful services. If you prefer to seek help away from campus, the VA website (www.va.gov) can help you find VA resources in your area.

QUICK TERM

Traumatic brain injury (TBI): an injury that occurs when a force traumatizes the brain, resulting in loss of consciousness, altered mental state, and/or a loss of memory about the event.

Veterans Clubs and Organizations

Check to see if your school has a Veterans Center. If so, it can be a place to hang out and talk with other students like yourself. You can share "war stories" and experiences. You can also profitably learn about what classes you may want to take, which instructors are interesting or especially understanding of military students, and what resources or activities your school offers. Ask other military students, too, about military-oriented clubs and organizations.

Learn to network with local and national military connections to find support services. Try social networking sites, such as Facebook (www.facebook.com) and LinkedIn (www.linkedin.com), to expand your existing group of contacts.

Student Veterans of America

An increasing number of schools have their own chapters of the Student Veterans of America (www.studentveterans.org). The mission of this national or-

ganization is: "To provide military veterans with the resources, support, and advocacy needed to succeed in higher education and following graduation."

Other National Military Organizations

You can also consider the American Legion (www.legion.org), Veterans of Foreign Wars (www.vfw.org), or other national military organizations with local chapters. While you may think such organizations are for older veterans from the Vietnam era and earlier, membership has changed since the prolonged wars in Iraq and Afghanistan. You might find potential friends your own age or job leads in the local posts; you have nothing to lose by checking them out. The Legion also offers a wealth of educational information on its website, such as its long-running Need a Lift (www.legion.org/mygibill/needalift).

ROTC Programs

If your school has a ROTC program, stop by the detachment and meet the cadre and students. You might be able to share some of your expertise with the students, and the cadre will probably be glad to see you. ROTC detachments are often understaffed and may feel a bit alienated. Veterans and active duty military students can provide welcome relief as well as volunteer resources. In return, you can meet new friends, help with a worthwhile endeavor, and get information that can help you in class.

Additional Resources

Many additional resources exist—on the Web, on campus, or in the college library. Let's wrap up with additional resources that are likely to be of interest.

Local

Beyond the normal administrative information about school policies, registration schedules, faculty information, tuition, and fees—look for resources that can help you become a better student. The school library is a good place to start. Locate the library website and investigate the tools available to help you with research, writing, tutoring services, test taking, and study tips. If these tools are not in the library, look for them elsewhere; there may be a place called a Teaching and Learning Center, Studies Center, or something similar. If you can't find them, ask your instructor or other students.

Other possibilities include the following:

- If your school does not have a physical Veterans Center, it may have a virtual one in cyberspace. At the least, you should be able to find—or, if necessary, start—a related veterans or military student group on Facebook or other social networking site.
- Near a military base? Check out the resources they may have to help you. The base website can be a good place to start. Most bases have a library and a base education center.
- State government websites can also be enlightening. Many states have special resources and programs for veterans who reside in the state.

National

External Web resources may also be useful for military members and veterans, but be careful. Check the credentials of the site's sponsor. Ask advisors, the Education Service Officer (ESO), or campus librarian if you have any doubts about the source. Here are some helpful, reliable sites to get you started:

- Career resources for military vets: Corporate Gray (www.corporate-gray.com), Helmets to Hardhats (helmetstohardhats.org), and Recruit-Military (recruitmilitary.com).

- National Center for PTSD (www.ptsd.va.gov).

- Brain Injury Association of America (www.biausa.org).

- National Association Veterans Upward Bound (www.navub.org/page/VUB-Program-Information).

- How to Take on College Studying: Visit www.collegeboard.com and search for "college studying."

Chapter 5
Life After Graduation

ONCE YOU HAVE ACCOMPLISHED YOUR EDUCATIONAL GOAL and earned your college degree, what's next? If you start planning your career search during college, you will be better equipped to hunt for and find the best job possible.

To help you prepare now for the all-important job hunt, this chapter focuses on building and maintaining networks, developing a strong resume, and engaging in lifelong learning.

Building and Maintaining Networks

You have two communities to network with—your military family and your collegiate family of instructors, classmates, and alumni. Your challenge is to build and maintain those networks. Let's look at both communities.

Military Community

You can build a network of friends, colleagues, and experts by turning to on-campus military organizations. Look to people you have served with (former commanders are often especially proud of your educational accomplishments and may be willing to provide job recommendations), veteran faculty members, and fellow military students. Through these resources and contacts, you will also be able to target companies that actively recruit former and active duty military, especially those with specialized training requirements and security clearances.

Organizations such as the Military and Veteran Job Network (jobs.vetfriends.com/a/jobs/find-jobs) can also help with the job search. In addition, the Department of Defense, in coordination with the Department of Veterans Affairs and the Department of Labor, has established the Transition Assistance Program (TAP) to help separating military personnel.

If you're seeking a job with the federal government, being a veteran gives you an edge. Being a veteran can mean five extra points on a points-based employment application—and five more points if you are disabled.

> **Transition Assistance Program (TAP)**
>
> *TAP resources can help you find work, manage finances, write a resume, prepare for a job interview, get relocation assistance, and more. Veterans and member of the Guard and Reserves can access its services. For more information, see the TAP website (www.turbotap.org/portal/transition/resources/About_Us).*

School Community

Often, the best way to get a job interview is through word of mouth. If you've been active in organizations during college or worked with others in class, let your colleagues, instructors, and friends know what your job aims are. Ask for suggestions about who they might know in the field you want to pursue. You may be surprised. A friend may know others who would be willing to talk to you about their jobs, what they do day to day, and how they found work. Some of your instructors may work in jobs that interest you—talk to them to find out. They might even be willing to set you up with a job interview or give you the name of a valuable contact. Also, use the career services offices at your school—and use them early and often.

As your authors can attest, jobs and advancement often come from those you know or those who have common interests—like your branch of service or places where you were stationed. While you were taking college courses, you also encountered other students and faculty members who were interested in the same subjects you were taking. Don't let your relationships with those people dissolve when you graduate. Stay in contact through e-mails, telephone calls, social networking, and activities. Consider these tips for keeping your relationships strong:

- Maintain the ties to military and veterans' organizations you cultivated during college.
- Join your school's alumni organization. Sign up to receive alumni newsletters, attend activities, serve on committees, or even run for elected office.
- Consider LinkedIn, Facebook, or other Web 2.0 communities. Keep your personal profile current and professional. Actively participate in discussions, but remember that potential employers may review your posts or tweets.
- Join professional organizations, and consider attending their conferences and meetings. Join committees, run for office, and help plan or organize activities. Membership or holding an office in such organizations may distinguish your resume.
- Stay in touch by sending cards for holidays or special occasions. Remember to try to contact your favorite instructors and professional contacts at conferences or other events.

Building an Effective Personnel Record and Resume

Once you have your degree in hand, how can you get the most from it? Active duty military should focus on their personnel records, and veterans need to develop their resumes.

Active Duty and Reservists

Update your educational status in your personnel records as soon as possible. Why? A college degree may be required for promotion. At the very least, it makes you more competitive for selection to the next rank. Visit your personnel office with a copy of your diploma and academic transcript, and make sure the clerk updates your records accurately.

Hint

Try to hold on to security clearances as long as possible. "Short-timers" may want to consider talking to potential employers before leaving the service to maximize any security clearance advantage.

Veterans

To pursue a job, make sure you have formal documentation of your military service and the transcripts or diploma to show the degrees you've earned. In addition, develop a strong resume that will serve as your main calling card during a job search. Here are some additional tips:

- **Turn to your college for help.** Many colleges and universities offer career counseling services, including resume assistance. Use their services to help write your resume, then polish it and return for a critique. Get as much help as you can.
- **Develop different versions of your resume that you can tailor for different employment opportunities and employers.** For instance, some employers insist on an electronic resume, whereas others prefer a hard copy. Get prepared ahead of time by developing both. Target the wording in your resume to the specific job you are seeking.
- **Update and develop your social networking profile.** Do this on sites specifically designed for professional networking, such as LinkedIn. Your electronic presence can act as a source of job opportunities and can expose you to employment contacts.

Resumes

To build a strong resume, gather information about the job you're seeking and develop a clear objective, as shown in Figure 5-1. Gear your objective to the job you're seeking. You can state your employment objective in a cover letter that forwards your resume to the potential employer, or in the body of the resume itself.

FIGURE **5-1** | **Sample Objective Statements for Resume or Cover Letter**

Objective: To teach first, second, or third grade in an inner city school.

Objective: To obtain an entry-level claims officer position in a health insurance company.

Objective: To work as an office manager for a small- to medium-sized law firm.

Objective: To work as an account manager at ACME Financial Services.

Resumes are visual documents. Make sure that they look nice and give a professional impression. Tailor your resume to meet the needs of your prospective employer so that it's easy to understand how you fit the job. Read the job application and specifications carefully to discover key terms that you should use to indicate that you meet the qualifications—especially when applying for a job that uses automated resume-screening devices.

Most resumes have several sections: educational and work experience, skills and abilities, awards and honors, professional memberships, and references. Be sure to describe your military job experience in terms a civilian employer can understand. The "Military to Civilian Occupation Translator" offered by Career One Stop (www.careerinfonet.org/moc/), a website sponsored by the Department of Labor, can help. Finally, keep your resume short, readable, well-organized, and error-free. Sample resumes and writing tips can be found on the TAP website.

Resume Alert

You usually want to include your military service in a resume, but be careful not to embellish. Listing unearned decorations, combat experience that you did not have, or any other form of inaccurate information on a resume is often grounds for dismissal from your job.

Lifelong Learning

Learning shouldn't stop just because you've earned your degree. Not only is continuing to study important for your intellectual health, but the world is an ever-changing place. Keeping up with the latest information is a necessary part of being a responsible adult.

You may want to consider earning an advanced degree. A bachelor's degree does not carry the same weight today that it did years ago, and a master's or doctoral degree will set you that much farther apart from the pack.

Also, consider professional development courses and certifications in your field. If you completed your degree in accounting or finance, for example, you may want to study for the Certified Public Accountant (CPA) exam. Beyond your college degree, such credentials can be important in career advancement. If you are on active duty, you may be able to use tuition assistance funds for your graduate degree. Check with your Education Services Officer (ESO). GI Bill funds can be used for graduate degrees and even professional certificate programs.

Socrates said, "The only good is knowledge and the only evil is ignorance." You have chosen the path of knowledge, which demands hard work and discipline. Earning a college degree provides evidence that you have the dedication, intelligence, and motivation to reach your goals, and that you have the strength of character to lead and to follow. Use your degree as a stepping stone to the next goal, and set your goals high. No matter what you do after college, you will be better for the knowledge you have gained through your studies.

"In the long run, men only hit what they aim at."

Henry David Thoreau, Walden, 1854

Notes